# Guac Off!

# Guac Off!

Rules and Recipes for Becoming
Guacamole Champion of the World

by Nathan Myers
Photographs by Jeremiah Webster

**CHRONICLE BOOKS**

SAN FRANCISCO

Library of Congress Cataloging-in-Publication Data available.

ISBN 978-0-8118-6506-7

Manufactured in China.

Designed by Suzanne LaGasa

10 9 8 7 6 5 4 3 2

Chronicle Books LLC
680 Second Street
San Francisco, California 94107

www.chroniclebooks.com

*For Fallbrook*

# Contents

# The Love You Make

A nutritious snack and legendary aphrodisiac—there's an undeniable magic that surrounds guacamole. Just look at the way people gather around a bowl, bumping chips to grab some gorgeous green goodness. That's what this book is about: *Guac Off!* is more than just tasty avocado recipes, it's about the togetherness guacamole creates wherever it is made.

Growing up in Fallbrook, California, the "Avocado Capital of the World," we made guacamole the way Old West gunfighters cleaned their pistols: a casual act of tremendous consequence. In the ripening season, avocados would just come rolling down the road as my friends and I would be walking home from school. We'd pick up two for an easy and delicious after-school snack, and check the fridge when we got home. "Hmmm, applesauce, olives, hot sauce . . . yeah, I can make guac from that."

Our Gauc Offs started largely by accident: a late-summer argument over whose version of our native snack was most delectable. Before we knew it, judges were appointed, spectators gathered, and samples entered. The rest, as they say, is history, and a new tradition was born. The beauty of the tradition was (and still is), it didn't matter who won, Guac-ing Off was just fun.

And as our goofball ritual of guacamole shoot-outs became an anticipated annual gathering, we saw more and more "competitors" expressing themselves through unique and delicious recipes. It was a treat to watch friends joyously devouring each and every bowl down to the last lip-smacking dip, and we realized how much these traditions mattered. And why shouldn't they? In the same way avocados bring ingredients together, they bring people together, too. They are an amazing fruit exploding with nutrition, adaptable from soups to salads to smoothies, and even as a delicious butter substitute. Best of all, you can eat them all on their own.

We did a bit of research and found other people doing the same thing, even using the same silly name. Guac Offs were spontaneously sprouting up all over the place. The winner of our first Guac Off, El Primero (page 44), remains a local favorite. And many others from nearly a decade of Guac-ing Off—some winners, some crowd pleasers, some personal favorites—form the foundation of this book's recipe collection.

This is a book about expressing unconditional love for an amazing and unique fruit. John Lennon, a great avocado lover, explained it best, about life, and about guac: "In the end," he wrote, "the love you take is equal to the love you make." Making guacamole is making love, so let's dip in together.

# Love Grenades and Testicle Sauce

## A BRIEF HISTORY OF GUACAMOLE COMBAT

Avocados are an ancient fruit, a delicacy among prehistoric megafauna herbivores who competed for territory around the rare trees. As these massive animals went extinct, there were no creatures large enough to consume and pass a fertilized seed (the way most seed bearing plants insure their survival). With no means to continue its propagation, the coveted dinosaur fruit was nearly doomed.

Fortunately, *homo sapiens* were similarly enamored with this unique fruit. Although they could neither swallow nor pass the seed, they began cultivating the trees as early as A.D. 900 (as evidenced by avocado-shaped pots found in Incan grave sites in northern Peru). Mayan mythology suggests the sacred fruits were reserved as a fertility enhancer for their queens (and with the fruit's high concentration of folate, they weren't far off), but more practical minds believe these progressive cultures were already experimenting with various mixtures of the precious green mash, adding chiles, tomatoes, and salt to create extravagant new tastes. As their experiments progressed, it was only a matter of time before these scattered tribal cultures grew territorial about their recipes. Some things never change.

Just as Christopher Columbus "discovered" America, Hernando Cortez "discovered" guacamole. In 1518 Cortez set forth to colonize the interior of Mexico with his six hundred soldiers. Local cuisine was simple, mostly maize, beans, and squash, accented with tomatoes and chiles. As the campaign passed through the region of Puebla, an early avocado mecca, they found locals combining ingredients with a strange, green mash, believed to be a powerful sexual stimulant.

Entering the heart of the Aztec nation, Cortez was greeted as a god and presented with riches, servants, and, also, more rich green sauce. While their primary motivations were monetary, Cortez and his men took keen note of the valued dish. The Aztecs called it *ahuacatlmole*, or "testicle sauce" (*ahuacat* means "testicle" in the Nahuatl dialect; *mole* means "sauce"). The name reflected the fruit's distinctive dangle from its tree, but also its potency as an aphrodisiac and fertility aid. While testicle sauce was primarily reserved for royalty, Cortez's men noticed some of the lower classes engaging in clandestine competitions to create the most potent concoctions. Tomatoes, chiles, and salt were standard ingredients, but more adventurous ahuacatl-mole makers would add cactus juice, grasshoppers, and *acocils* (local lake shrimp). Though glossed over by contemporary history, these were in fact the world's first Gauc Offs.

As the Spanish conquistadores loaded avocado saplings aboard their gold-laden galleons, the avocado (and its fabled testicle sauce) reached a critical turning point; it was about to go global.

Ancient sailing vessels were anything but culinary epicenters. After months at sea with no refrigeration, the principal cuisine among salty seamen was strong rum and rank ale. There were no dairy products aboard, scarce fruit, and hard-tack bread that turned rock solid within days. One of the sailors' few savory recourses, however, was the avocado. Known then as "midshipmen's butter," the tough skinned, slow-to-ripen fruit was among the few live foods that survived weeks at sea, remaining delicious, oily, and nutritious—a fine complement to old bread or fresh fish.

Midshipmen's butter became one of the world's great explorer foods. Over time, as the fruit visited countries that suited its delicate growing requirements, the avocado colonized new continents and bonded with local ingredients. Indonesians mixed it with milk, coffee, and sugar to make a sweet, cold drink. Nicaraguans, christening the avocado *palta*, stuffed it with cheese, then battered and baked it in a chili sauce. Colombians and Ecuadorians made soups; Brazilians, ice cream. The Japanese rolled avocado into sushi. In the Middle East, it was served with pita, and in South Africa the avocado commonly replaced butter. The French Caribbeans blended it with codfish, garlic, and coconut as a dip, while Jamaicans flavored it with lime juice and Scotch bonnet chiles for a scorching cold bisque. In each their own way, the many cultures of the world were reinventing guacamole.

But it was aboard the supply-depraved merchant ships that the mysterious tradition of guacamole competitions endured. With limited yet diverse ingredients aboard, sailors invented new guacamole combinations to accompany their brittle bread. Maritime legends tell of salted-rodent guacamole, gunpowder guacamole, and even an ill-omened albatross guac. In this way, the secret and manyfold path of guacamole ventured to the far edges of the world.

Like the many nationalities passing through Ellis Island at the turn of the twentieth century, avocados entered the United States with something of an identity crisis. President George Washington was the first to notably mention the fruit, writing of the strange "agovago pears" he encountered in Barbados.

Others called them alligator pears, butter pears, *aguacate*, and a common mispronunciation of the Spanish *agovago* as "avocado" (a *New York Times* article even printed a short series of "avocado pear recipes" in 1912). In 1924 a handful of California growers associated under the name Calavos and hosted a naming contest for their identity-confused crop, eventually settling on "Calavos pear." Meanwhile, the mishmashed mispronunciation "avocado" had already wandered into the Oxford English Dictionary. Cemented in print, the name stuck.

Concerned with their fruit's sexually impure background (during this period, women seen buying avocados were considered unchaste), Calavos growers began a series of bold marketing campaigns. First, they promoted the fruit as a cheap substitute for meat; then, during the diet-crazed '30s, as "the aristocrat of salad fruits." In the war-torn '40s, they dubbed avocados "grenades of glamour"; while the '50s featured tiki-themed displays for avocado-enriched suburban luaus. In the liberalized '60s and '70s, avocados were dubbed "the love fruit from California," while antiwar hippies peacefully scooped from their luscious "love grenades"; and the '80s boasted billboards of slender supermodels saying, "Would this body lie to you?"

All the while, Cinco de Mayo reigned as guacamole's personal holiday. But in the early '90s, avocado growers set their sights on making Super Bowl Sunday see green.

Among guacamole connoisseurs, the day before Super Bowl Sunday came to be known as Avo-Bowl Saturday. On this day, guac makers designed themed guacamoles using the colors and native ingredients of the Super Bowl teams (black beans and jalapeños for the Oakland Raiders, shrimp and peppers for Tampa Bay, crab for San Francisco, and so on). Guacamole experts judged the dueling dips to divine which team would win the big game. Oddly, the guac was right more often than not.

The avocado growers' gamble paid off: By 1993, 10 million pounds of guacamole were consumed on game day. By 2003, CBS News reported that some 40 million pounds of guacamole had been consumed—"enough to cover an entire football field twelve feet deep" in guac.

The Avo-Bowl disappeared that year, slinking quietly away from the awkward limelight of guac-covered gridiron. Meanwhile, another form of guacamole contest began its revival in backyard barbecues all across America: the ancient tradition of pitting personal recipes against each other, similar to the Aztecs and ancient mariners. Uncomplicated by the stadium-sized hype of mass media and marketing, local underground Guac Offs endured as they began: communal gatherings of good friends and good food, joined in playful competition. Primal. Joyful. Delicious.

# The Code of the Guacamole Fighter

## A GUIDE TO GUAC-ING OFF

> *"To win without fighting is best."*
> —Sun Tzu, *The Art of War*

Guac Offs are deadly serious business. Reputations are won and lost and bragging rights defy the bounds of linear time. Too much lime or too little salt—the slightest decision—can alter the entire course of your life. Okay, maybe not. Nevertheless, the time-honored tradition of hosting a guacamole combat ceremony must be conducted with appropriate degrees of dignity and reverence.

- Silly hats should be worn on an "as needed" basis.

- Lewd behavior should be moderately ignored.

- Pre-guac smack talk should be limited to anonymous phone calls and absurd text messaging.

- Face-to-face confrontation should be reserved for day-of festivities, and, then, administered with exaggerated decorum.

In accordance with the ancient (and never-before-published) Code of the Guacamole Fighter, the following guidelines are structured around the five central imperatives of Sun Tzu's wildly adaptable treatise on confrontation, *The Art of War.* They are the Way, the Weather, the Terrain, the Leadership, and the Discipline.

Sun Tzu says: "The Way means inducing the people to have the same aim as the Leadership, so that they will share death and share life, without fear of danger."

The term "Guac Off" says a lot. It is strangely self-explanatory, given that you won't find it in any dictionary—yet. It is both challenging and ridiculous, announcing a competition that is really not a competition at all. Whether you hand-deliver written taunts, blast a group e-mail, or employ an online service like Evite.com or Socializr.com, the tone of your challenge is critical.

It's simple enough to write:

## We're Guac-ing Off

**Rules**: Limit of two avocados per entry. Otherwise, anything goes.

**Stakes**: One bottle of fine tequila and the title of Master Guac-maker.

**Party runs from (time) to (time)**, with the judging beginning promptly at (time). BYOB. Dinner provided. Desserts and appetizers encouraged.

Honor and respect to all who accept this challenge.

Bring your best guac—this ain't no Tupperware party.

RSVP to (contact info).

Understatement is the key. Throw down the gauntlet and let bewilderment handle the rest. People know what a Guac Off is, even if they don't. This is the Way.

## THE WEATHER

Sun Tzu says: "The Weather means the seasons."

Ripe avocados ensure a good Guac Off. These days, thanks to staggered growing seasons and the year-round nature of Hass avos, quality avocados are almost always available. Check with your local grocer if you have doubts about your area.

Guac Offs are best conducted in the afternoon, prior to dinner. Outdoors in warm weather is always preferable, so that as the competition concludes the barbecue is just firing up and the patient palates of all assembled can sample the array of guacs while tacos take shape and margaritas find their mark. By sunset, every guest should have two tacos in their belly and be quietly considering a third.

## THE TERRAIN

Sun Tzu says: "The Terrain is to be assessed in terms of distance, difficulty, or ease of travel, dimension, and safety."

Proper setup ensures that the host is able to enjoy the event as well. Set aside a neat table for the Guac Off entries, decorated, perhaps, with the raw munitions of guacamole: avos, chiles, tomatoes, onions, and garlic. Have some room in the fridge, or a designated cooler, to house competing guacamoles until the competition starts. Remember, guests arrive at a Guac

Off anxious to devour guacamole, so place a large bowl of non-comp "goalie guac" in a defensive position to divert the hungry mob from compromising the competitors' entries.

Every Guac Off also needs a master of ceremonies. The master of ceremonies should have good crowd-control and organizational abilities. The master of ceremonies may not compete in the Guac Off.

All official entries need to sign in with the appointed master of ceremonies prior to the event (dignified titles like Smashamacoli, Guac-a-Doodle-Doo, and Guac 'n' Roll are encouraged). Place all registered guacs in identical, numbered bowls to discourage bribery of, or favoritism from, the judges.

Appoint food-savvy judges prior to the day of the event. Each judge should arrive with his or her preferred brand of chip and know the evaluation criteria. Standard guacamole-judging criteria include presentation, texture, and taste (a scale of 1 to 5 for each category works well). There may also be side awards for Most Unique and Most Beautiful. The master of ceremonies must meet with the judges prior to the competition start to review the criteria, and remind them to exhibit great levels of sophistication and aptitude when performing their task.

Once the judging is complete, the master of ceremonies announces the winner and presents the prize (accompanied by shot glasses, salt, and lime wedges). Only then may everyone else begin to sample (i.e. shamelessly devour) the assembled guacamoles. Tradition holds that the winner should immediately dedicate victory shots with his or her fellow competitors from the prize bottle and make a short, boastful speech. (Note: Any Guac Off at which the prize bottle leaves the contest grounds intact *must* be considered null and void.)

The first bowl finished on the competitor's table is considered The People's Choice. This is very honorable, if anyone remembers or cares by that point.

Sun Tzu says: "Leadership is a matter of intelligence, trustworthiness, humanity, courage, and sternness."

In accordance with the Code of the Guacamole Fighter, the host of any guacamole combat sets forth with no intention of winning at their own event. However, they should approach the event with the wily ferocity of a cornered tiger. Their guacamole should be extreme in nature, drawing significant attention but ultimately failing to appease the judges' delicate palates.

The real victory is that everyone enjoys themselves, and the winning guac-maker gives everyone something to talk about until the following year . . . if they can wait that long.

Sun Tzu says: "Disciple means organization, chain of command, and logistics."

Let's put our chips aside for a moment and be frank: A Guac Off is a fun and entertaining excuse to get together with friends and family. It is food and drink, and something to laugh about along the way. And after the "competition," there's loads of delicious and creative guacamole for everyone to gobble up.

If you are well prepared for your Guac Off, you'll be able to sit back and enjoy the ride. And if you approach it with the appropriate level of lightheartedness, it will become an event people remember fondly and look forward to attending again. Traditions, like food, bring people together.

Scholars of Sun Tzu's *The Art of War* noted that the text was actually a treatise against war. Master Sun employs the brutality and inhumanity of war as a motivation to avoid it. Similarly, the art of fighting with food—be it guacamole combat or chili cook-offs—is ultimately about the love of food; contestants share the inspiration of their recipes while appreciating the creativity of their opponents'.

And yes, this is getting a bit philosophical for a book about guacamole, but perhaps some remnant of this heady whim will come to mind after that third shot of tequila, and you'll mumble something vaguely worldly and largely befuddling to those gathered with you about how guacamole fighting really brings people together.

And when they stare back at you in blank confusion, just say, "But next time, you're all going down."

# Persea Americana Fabuloso

## USEFUL INFO ABOUT AVOCADOS

Good guacamole comes from good avocados. It's as simple as that. So let's take a moment to understand this versatile fruit, as it will provide the foundation for everything that follows in this book.

Any grower will tell you that avocados are a demanding fruit. They are sensitive to cold, heat, moisture, dryness, fog, intense sun . . . you name it. They insist on being handpicked before they deign to ripen. Once picked, avocados transition rapidly from unripe to overripe. And once cut open, they quickly begin to brown. The fact is, avocados require human love. Without humans cultivating avocados, their oversized seeds would not be able to fertilize and the slow-rooting trees would surely become extinct. The merits of avocados' rich, buttery flesh, of which humans can't get enough, ensure their continued prosperity. And for those willing to cultivate, the reward surpasses the challenge.

An avocado's flesh is unlike that of any other fruit: it is nutty and oily instead of sweet; firm enough to slice, yet spreadable like butter; and it blends or pairs neatly with a variety of foods. Its covalent creaminess binds otherwise disparate ingredients like some miraculous dressing, transforming unstable structures (such as corn, onions, and mango) into tasty concoctions. It is used in high-end shampoos and Hollywood spas, and for building Native American adobe houses.

To top it all off, avocados are extremely healthful:

- Ounce for ounce, avocados contain more protein, fiber, potassium, magnesium, folate, thiamin, niacin, and riboflavin than any of the other fruits that made the "top twenty most commonly eaten fruits" list.

- Avocados are rich in vitamins A, C, E, and K, with 60 percent more potassium than bananas, 10 percent of the daily intake of iron required for adults, and as much fiber as whole wheat bread or corn on the cob.

- Avocados are naturally free of cholesterol and sodium, which makes them a healthful alternative to butter, sour cream, and mayonnaise.

- Research has shown avocados to be "nutrient boosters," meaning they allow the body to absorb more heart-healthy, cancer-fighting nutrients like alpha- and beta-carotene.

- Avocados are rich in lutein, a natural antioxidant that is concentrated in the macula of the eye, which, research suggests, helps maintain healthy eyesight. An ounce of avocado contains 81 micrograms of lutein.

- As an avocado ripens, the saturated palmitic acid decreases and the monounsaturated oleic acid increases (i.e., it becomes better for you). Many studies have concurred on the specific dietary benefits of monounsaturated fat for both health promotion and disease prevention.

- Avocado oils are good for your skin and hair (which is why they're used in high-end shampoos and facial masks).

- And, yes, a single avocado packs over 300 calories and 15 percent of the FDA's recommended daily amount of fat, but it's primarily monounsaturated fat, "the good fat." In fact, avocados have been noted for their antibacterial and anti-inflammatory properties, and are believed to have curative effects on such ailments as diarrhea, dysentery, abdominal pain, and high blood pressure.

But mostly, they just taste really, really good.

# Avocado Quick Facts

## TREES AND CULTIVATION

Avocado trees, *Persea americana*, require the deep, well-aerated soils and mild tropical climate conditions found in areas like southern Spain, South Africa, Peru, central and northern Chile, Vietnam, Indonesia, the Philippines, Australia, New Zealand, Central America, Mexico, and the United States. Ninety-five percent of the U.S. avocado production is from California, with 80 percent of that in San Diego county (including the small town of Fallbrook, the "Avocado Capital of the World"). The trees have a long juvenile period, and most originate from grafting of proven varieties onto hearty rootstock.

The trees can grow up to sixty to seventy feet and yield up to five hundred fruits per season, though average production is closer to one hundred fifty to two hundred fruits per season. Fruits must fully mature on the tree to ripen properly, but will not begin to ripen until off the tree. Once picked, avocados ripen in a few days at room temperature (faster if stored with other fruits, slower if stored in cool temperatures).

## TYPES AND AVAILABILITY

There are hundreds of types of avocados, all descended from three primary subspecies: the West Indian, Guatemalan, and Mexican. However, only a few types are commercially marketed, and while any avocado will suffice for making guacamole, some are better than others. Here, in order of preference, are a few to look for:

**Hass:** This pebbly black, pear-shaped, Guatemalan-Mexican hybrid accounts for three quarters of all avocados sold in the United States and is the undisputed champ of the guacamole world. Every single Hass tree is a descendent of a single seed planted by U.S. postal worker Rudolph Hass in 1926. Guac-makers mourned when the legendary mother tree finally died of root rot in 2002, but its many generations of grafting represent more than 80 percent of all avocado trees in Mexico and the United States today. Not only is their yellow-green flesh particularly rich and oily, but the fruits also have a tough skin so they ship and store well, and they can be harvested in all seasons, making the Hass desirable to both grower and consumer alike. Best season: spring to fall (but available all year).

**Fuerte:** Big and round, rich and nutty, Fuertes were the dominant pre-Hass avocados after they survived the harsh frost of 1913 that wiped out most other U.S. strains (hence their name, which means "strong" in Spanish). The hearty, yellow-gold flesh of Fuertes is the filet mignon of avocado, but their thin skin makes them less desirable for packing and storing. Best season: fall to spring.

**Lamb Hass:** This recent relative of the Hass weighs in bigger and comes into season later (an advantage to U.S. growers, who stagger their season with Latin American and Mexican growers), but purists maintain that the original Hass is still tastier than the Lamb. It's a top contender either way. Best season: spring to fall.

**Gwen:** Another new Hass hybrid (first grown in 1982), Gwens yield a gold-green flesh that stays fresh longer than that of other varieties and is rich and creamy like homemade butter. Best season: late winter to midsummer.

**Reed:** Big, shiny summertime cannonballs, Reed avocados yield plenty of smooth, creamy flesh, but are not quite as nutty or rich as the other varieties. Best season: summer to fall.

Other notable avocados include Pinkerton, Bacon, and Zutano, which are delicious in their own right, but not quite comparable to Hass or Fuerte for guac-making.

## RIPENESS

Ripeness is crucial to guacamole. A ripe avocado will yield to gentle pressure when squeezed. The inner flesh should be yellow-green or yellow-gold when ripe. The flesh oxidizes and turns brown quickly after exposure to air, so add a squeeze of lime or lemon juice to a peeled avocado, cover it, and store it in your refrigerator to prevent browning. Good avocado flesh should be a lively, bright green and soft like butter. Unripe avocado flesh is yellow and firm. If an avocado has brown spots inside, simply cut them away and use the yellow and green parts.

## STORAGE

Store avocados in a cool environment and away from direct sunlight. You can store them alone or with other fruit. They usually ripen three to five days after picking (depending on storage, maturity, and type). To quickly ripen a raw avocado, store it in a paper bag with another fruit, such as an apple. To slow ripening, refrigerate it (but never freeze). Store guacamole in an airtight container in the refrigerator until discoloration appears. Don't worry, guacamole will survive several hours completely exposed, and a day or two in the fridge. Once it begins to brown, throw it out and start over.

## PORTION

One large avocado yields about 1 cup of flesh (smaller varieties yield closer to ¾ cup).

## COOKING AND HANDLING

Open avocados as close to eating as possible. Cooking generally ruins their flavor and turns them bitter. Serve them fresh and raw.

## VOODOO LOVE MOJO

Ancient guac makers cherished avocados as an aphrodisiac. Modern scientists have proven their enormous health benefits. Chefs from every culture employ their rich, creamy flesh in a panoply of recipes, from sushi to ice creams. From Mayan mythology and Aztec etymology to modern marketing and hippie hoo-haw, avocados are love fruit. And the mishmash messenger called guacamole is their Cupid. However you look at it, avocados are a potent and versatile ingredient bursting with health, flavor, and glamour.

Now, let's make some guac.

# Mashing and Folding

## THE JOY OF GUAC-ING

Guacamole is a pleasure. Among other appetizers, a well-made guac will put fatty sour creams, gassy bean dips, and salty nut bowls to shame. And it's just so easy to make. Like a good roll in the hay, once you know a few simple tricks the rest is fun to figure out on your own. If guacamole is the food of love, then this chapter is the *Kama Sutra* for avocados. And in a similar way, we recommend studying the manual beforehand, then putting it aside during the act. Keep it simple and fresh, and share it with the people you love.

### THE PERFECT GUAC KNIFE

It's called a *spatula spreader*—a knife commonly used for making sandwiches. The sharp, serrated edge slices ingredients well, while its rounded tip traces the inside edges of the avocado skin. Your dicing crosshatch cuts will slice to the skin without penetrating it, and your scooping will scrape off every last bit of the ripest flesh near the skin of the avocado. Other knives work fine, but the spatula spreader works divine.

## THE PERFECT GUAC BOWL

The traditional *molcajete* (mortar) and *tejolote* (pestle) were the world's first food processors, wonderful for mashing, grinding, preparing, and even serving everything guac-related. The stone bowl can be soaked in water to keep food cool or heated in an oven to keep food warm. Its porous nature famously transferred lingering flavors from one dish to the next, which sounds a bit . . . gross. Unsanitary, even. Traditional mortars are impossible to clean perfectly. They are also incredibly heavy, and the rough stone is highly prone to chipping (not to mention breaking your chips). So if you're hosting a cooking show on the Travel Channel, guac-ing in a big, stone molcajete will surely juice your street cred. Otherwise, just use something medium-sized, bright, smooth, and sterile. Mix in one, serve in another, and smile like Martha Stewart while you do it.

## CUTTING INTO AVOCADOS

There is a perfect way to slice an avocado, so pay attention: Starting just beside the stem, insert your knife down to the seed and halve the avocado lengthwise, cutting down to the seed around the entire circumference of the fruit. Gently twist and pull the two halves completely apart—the seed will remain neatly in one side. Lightly stick your knife into the seed, twist slightly, and it should pull out easily. Crosshatch the flesh down to the inner skin, making ½-inch cubes on each side. Use a spoon or the edge of your spatula spreader to scrape the cubed flesh away from the skin directly into your bowl. When an avocado is ripe, these fleshy cubes will be about the perfect consistency for guacamole (a less ripe avocado may need some mashing with a fork). They will naturally degrade as you mix in other ingredients, but try to keep your guac nice and chunky.

## CHOPPING THE OTHER INGREDIENTS

Sizing of ingredients is all personal preference. Generally, bright, colorful ingredients (peppers, tomatoes, mangos) should be cut larger (¼- to ½-inch cubes) while greenish, flavoring ingredients (onions, garlic, cilantro) should be finely diced.

## MEASURING THE OTHER INGREDIENTS

Measuring is no fun. And guac-ing must be fun. Guac is about feeling your way to bold new creations. For the purposes of this book, portions have been approximated for all the recipes to set you on the proper path of guac-ing. However, once you get the hang of things, take off your lab coat and live a little. It will be okay.

## TIMING GUAC

There is a rhythm to making guacamole. Make your guac as close to eating it as possible, but an hour or two worth of chill time in the refrigerator is also good to firm and enhance flavors.

## MASHING AND FOLDING

The love you take is equal to the love you make. Each cut. Each shake. Each stir. It all matters. That being said, every guac is unique, and it is not for any book to dictate how you should mix or shake or chop. Just be mindful of the shape, size, and consistency of your accoutrements. It's easy to add more, but difficult to take back. Finally, how you stir your ingredients together— whether you mash boldly with a rugged fork or fold gently with a gilded butter knife—will reflect how your flavors blend together or stand apart.

Rounds, triangles, strips, or scoops. White corn, yellow corn, flour tortilla, or baked veggie. Hint of Lime, Restaurant Style, Bite Size Gold, or Sizzlin' Picante. Addressing the market's dizzying array of chips is enough to make your head spin. Do you grab blindly? Go for bulk? Submit to the name brand? Up to you. We recommend keeping your chips as simple as possible: buy local brands; support nearby restaurants; and for sanctioned Guac Offs, provide a selection of shapes, flavors, and colors to inspire experimentation and celebrate diversity. With chips about $2 a bag, you can afford to pretend that it matters a lot.

In a traditional Guac Off, all guacamoles should be presented in identical vessels to prevent foul play or aesthetic victories. However, in the real world, presentation is an essential element of every guacamole. Pineapple guacs can be served in scooped-out pineapples, or a spicy Fresno chile guac in a bell pepper shell. Classic guacs should favor bright Mexican bowls or dip-friendly chip-carriages. With themed and regional guacs, garnish your final product with a dash of indigenous ingredients, decorate with flags, umbrellas, or plastic action figures, and use serving dishes that enhance the motif of your guac. Be creative. Get weird. And serve with love.

*recipes for*

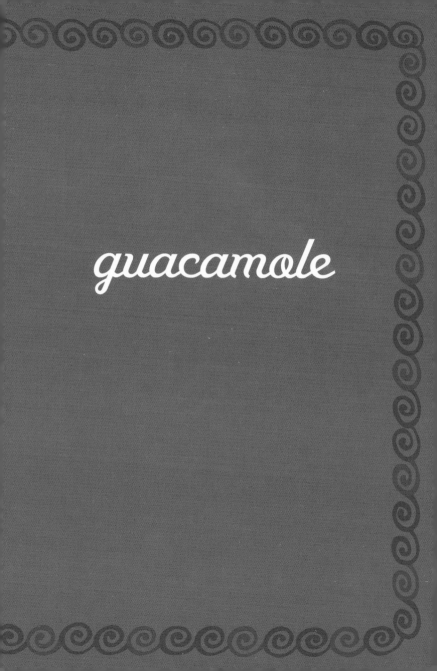

guacamole

classic guacs

Simple is simple. As your guac-ing skills improve, you'll feel the urge to add more ingredients. Don't. Classic guacamoles are founded on the pairing of a few essential flavors.

# Simple Guac

*Avocado. Lime. Salt. These three simple ingredients are all you need to make guacamole. You can even serve this guac right in its own skin and never dirty a dish.*

2 large avocados, diced
(about 2 cups)

Juice of 1 lime (about
2 tablespoons)

Salt

**Tortilla chips**

*Makes about 2 cups*

**In a medium bowl,** combine the avocados and lime juice with a large fork. Mash together to form a chunky mixture. Season to taste with salt. Serve immediately with tortilla chips.

# Brooktown Classic

## (Winner: 2003)

*Almost half of California's $300-million-a-year avocado crop comes from the tiny North County San Diego town of Fallbrook. This is how we roll in the Avocado Promised Land.*

2 large avocados, diced
(about 2 cups)

Juice of 2 limes (about ¼ cup)

One 4-ounce can diced green
chiles, drained

1 Roma tomato, diced

2 cloves garlic, minced
(about 2 teaspoons)

2 tablespoons finely diced
white onion

1 tablespoon finely chopped
cilantro

Salt

Pepper

Hot sauce

Tortilla chips

*Makes about 2 cups*

**In a medium bowl,** combine the avocados and lime juice with a large fork. Mash together to form a chunky mixture. Stir in the chiles, tomato, garlic, onion, and cilantro. Season to taste with salt, pepper, and hot sauce. Serve immediately with tortilla chips.

# Spicy Jalapeño Guac

## (Winner: 2007)

*Jalapeños form a sublime union with avocados. Their heat naturally complements the creaminess of avocados.*

2 large avocados, diced (about 2 cups)

Juice of 2 limes (about ¼ cup)

2 jalapeño peppers, seeded and chopped

2 cloves garlic, minced

½ cup diced Roma tomato

½ cup finely chopped white onion

¼ cup finely chopped cilantro

Salt

Cayenne pepper

**Tortilla chips**

*Makes about 2 cups*

**In a medium bowl,** combine the avocados and lime juice with a large fork. Mash together to form a chunky mixture. Stir in the jalapeño, garlic, tomato, onion, and cilantro. Season to taste with salt and cayenne. Serve immediately with tortilla chips.

# El Primera

## (Winner: 2000)

*The winner of our first Guac Off simply cannot be ignored. The trick is to mix in the fresh Simple Salsa at the end. Make some extra salsa to serve on the side.*

2 large avocados, diced
(about 2 cups)

Juice of 2 limes (about ¼ cup)

2 cloves garlic, minced

1 tablespoon finely chopped
cilantro

2 tablespoons finely chopped
white onion

1 small jalapeño pepper, seeded
and finely chopped

½ cup Simple Salsa (facing page)

Salt

Pepper

**Tortilla chips**

*Makes about 2½ cups*

**In a medium bowl,** combine the avocados and lime juice with a large fork. Mash together to form a chunky mixture. Stir in the garlic, cilantro, onion, and jalapeño. Fold in the Simple Salsa. Season to taste with salt and pepper. Serve immediately with tortilla chips and the leftover Simple Salsa on the side.

# Simple Salsa

2 Roma tomatoes, chopped

2 green onions, finely chopped

1 tablespoon finely chopped
cilantro

2 cloves garlic, minced

*Makes 1 cup*

**In a small bowl,** mix together the tomato, green onions, cilantro, and garlic with a wooden spoon.

# Mango Guac

*The mango and avocado are kissing cousins, constantly competing for the title of World's Sexiest Fruit. Putting them together should be X-rated.*

2 large avocados, diced
(about 2 cups)

1 large mango, peeled, seeded,
and cut into ½-inch cubes
(about ½ cup)

Juice of 2 limes (about ¼ cup)

½ cup chopped red bell pepper

2 teaspoons finely chopped cilantro

¼ cup diced jicama

½ teaspoon ground cumin

Salt

Pepper

Tortilla chips

*Makes about 2½ cups*

**In a medium bowl,** combine the avocados, mango, and lime juice with a large fork. Mash together to form a chunky mixture. Stir in the bell pepper, cilantro, jicama, and cumin. Season to taste with salt and pepper. Serve immediately with tortilla chips.

# Southwestern Guac

*Colorful and tasty, this vibrant spin on guacamole also tastes amazing with fish, tacos, and quesadillas. Keep your avocado nice and chunky and fold gently with the other ingredients for the most aesthetic results.*

2 large avocados, diced
    (about 2 cups)

Juice of 1 lime (about
    2 tablespoons)

2 tablespoons canned corn, drained
    (or freshly cooked)

2 tablespoons canned black beans,
    drained

2 tablespoons chopped black olives

1 tablespoon finely chopped
    cilantro

1 tablespoon finely chopped
    red onion

1 clove garlic, minced

Salt

Pepper

**Tortilla chips**

*Makes about 2½ cups*

**In a medium bowl,** combine the avocados and lime juice with a large fork. Mash together to form a chunky mixture. Fold in the corn, black beans, olives, cilantro, red onion, and garlic. Season to taste with salt and pepper and fold again lightly to form a vibrant guacamole. Serve immediately with tortilla chips.

# Garlic Guac

*Garlic's potent versatility nearly rivals that of the avocado. Put the two together and you have a powerful force. Not everyone is keen on this much garlic, but for those of you who are, this delightfully pungent guac will make you swoon.*

2 large avocados, diced
   (about 2 cups)

Juice of 2 limes (about ¼ cup)

6 cloves garlic, minced

¼ cup chopped red bell pepper

¼ cup finely chopped cilantro

¼ cup finely chopped white onion

½ teaspoon finely chopped oregano

½ teaspoon finely chopped
   fresh thyme

Salt

Pepper

Hot sauce

**Tortilla chips**

*Makes about 3 cups*

**In a medium bowl,** combine the avocados, lime juice, garlic, bell pepper, cilantro, onion, oregano, and thyme with a large fork. Mash together to form a chunky mixture. Season to taste with salt, pepper, and hot sauce. Serve immediately with tortilla chips.

# Chunky Tomato Guac

*This gorgeous, colorful guac could serve as the centerpiece of your Mexican spread.*

2 large avocados, diced
   (about 2 cups)

Juice of 2 limes (about ¼ cup)

One 4-ounce can diced
   green chiles, drained

2 cloves garlic, minced

¼ cup finely diced yellow onion

Salt

Pepper

Hot sauce

½ cup cubed Roma tomato
   (about ½-inch cubes)

**Tortilla chips**

*Makes about 2 cups*

**In a medium bowl,** combine the avocados and lime juice with a large spoon. Stir in the chiles, garlic, and onion. Season to taste with salt, pepper, and hot sauce. Except for a few cubes, gently fold in the tomato. Sprinkle the remaining tomato over the top for garnish. Serve immediately with tortilla chips.

# Lemon Guac

*When life gives you lemons, make lemon guac.*

2 large avocados, diced
(about 2 cups)

Juice of 2 lemons (about ¼ cup)

2 tablespoons finely chopped
cilantro

½ cup finely chopped red onion

¼ cup seeded and chopped
jalapeño pepper

One 4-ounce can diced green chiles,
drained

Salt

Pepper

Hot sauce

**Tortilla chips**

*Makes about 3 cups*

**In a medium bowl,** combine the avocados and lemon juice with
a large spoon. Stir in the cilantro, onion, jalapeño, and green
chiles. Season to taste with salt, pepper, and hot sauce. Serve
immediately with tortilla chips.

# Party Guac

*Feed the herd. This is the seven-layer dip of the guac world—it turns two avocados into a hearty dip ideal for a big Game Day.*

2 large avocados, diced (about 2 cups)

Juice from 2 limes (about ¼ cup)

One 4-ounce can diced green chiles, drained

Salt

Pepper

Hot sauce

1 packet taco seasoning mix

1 cup sour cream

One 16-ounce can refried beans

½ cup grated Cheddar cheese

½ cup chopped black olives

½ cup shredded iceberg lettuce

½ cup diced Roma tomato

**Tortilla chips**

*Makes about 5½ cups*

**In a medium bowl,** combine the avocados, lime juice, and green chiles with a large spoon. Season to taste with salt, pepper, and hot sauce. Set aside. In a small bowl, stir together the taco seasoning mix and sour cream. Set aside. Warm the refried beans on the stove over medium heat for 5 minutes or in the microwave for 2 minutes on medium. Spread the warmed refried beans in the bottom of a 9-by-13-inch serving dish. Layer the Cheddar cheese over the beans, then, one over the other, layer the taco seasoning–sour cream mixture, the olives, lettuce, and tomato, and top off with the avocado mixture. Serve immediately with tortilla chips.

# Flaming Lips Habanero Guac

*On the spiciness scale, the yellow, orange, and red habanero chiles rank right up there at "leave the room crying"—a perfect 10. Use the red ones for maximum masochism. (Note: Liquids like beer don't cure spice burn—take something creamy, like yogurt, or suck on a lime, or eat a spoonful of sugar.)*

2 large avocados, diced
   (about 2 cups)

Juice of 2 lemons (about ¼ cup)

2 cloves garlic, minced

1 green onion, chopped

⅔ cup chopped Roma tomato

⅓ cup sour cream

2 tablespoons finely chopped
   cilantro

3 teaspoons minced
   fresh habanero chile

Salt

Pepper

**Tortilla chips**

*Makes about 3 cups*

**In a medium bowl,** combine the avocados, lemon juice, garlic, green onion, tomato, sour cream, cilantro, and chile with a large spoon. Season to taste with salt and pepper. Serve immediately with tortilla chips.

exotic guacs

Guacamole is one of the great world travelers. It can (and should) be made anywhere you find avocados. Bring your culinary discoveries home with you, too. The road runs both ways.

# Basque Guac

*Oil and vinegar, salt and pepper, garlic and onion—this is how they roll on the rugged coast of northern Spain. Bold and basic, simple and satisfying.*

2 large avocados, diced
(about 2 cups)

½ cup chopped Roma tomato

2 teaspoons olive oil

2 teaspoons balsamic vinegar

Salt

Pepper

**Tortilla chips**

*Makes about 2 cups*

**In a medium bowl,** combine the avocados, tomato, olive oil, and balsamic vinegar with a large spoon. Season to taste with salt and pepper. Serve immediately with tortilla chips.

# Asian Guac

*Technically, guacamole isn't of Asian persuasion, but once this recipe is out in the open, it will be. (Note: Check the Asian section of your local market for black sesame seeds, pickled ginger, wasabi powder, and pot sticker skins.)*

2 tablespoons black or white sesame seeds

2 large avocados, mashed (about 2 cups)

2 tablespoons shredded pickled ginger

1 teaspoon sugar

5 tablespoons seasoned rice vinegar or cider vinegar

1 teaspoon wasabi powder

**Pot Sticker Crisps (recipe follows)**

*Makes about 2 cups*

**Place the sesame seeds** in a 7- to 8-inch frying pan over medium-high heat, shaking often until seeds begin to pop (3 to 4 minutes). Watch carefully; the seeds go from toasted to burned quickly. Place the avocados in a medium bowl, and add the toasted seeds. Stir in the ginger, sugar, vinegar, and wasabi. Serve immediately with the Pot Sticker Crisps.

# Pot Sticker Crisps

Butter for greasing

12 round pot sticker skins (*gyoza*)

*Makes 12 crisps*

Preheat the oven to 450°F. Grease a 12-by-15-inch baking sheet with butter. Dip each pot sticker skin in a bowl of water, shaking off any excess. Lay in a single layer on the baking sheet. Bake until golden brown and crisp, 4 to 8 minutes. Transfer to cooling racks for 2 to 3 minutes. Serve warm with Asian Guac.

# High Desert Guac

*Bold. Boozy. And off the wall. Tequila-marinated juniper berries and prickly pear make this Sedona-born desert guac dangerously unique.*

¼ cup juniper berries

½ cup agave tequila

2 large avocados, diced (about 2 cups)

Juice from 2 limes (about ¼ cup)

¼ cup seeded and finely chopped jalapeño pepper

½ cup chilled prickly pear or mango salsa

Salt

**Corn chips**

*Makes about 2½ cups*

**Marinate the juniper berries** in the tequila overnight. Strain the tequila from the berries into a glass and reserve. Place the tequila-soaked berries in a mortar and mash with a pestle. In a medium bowl, combine the avocados, lime juice, jalapeño, pear salsa, and mashed juniper berries with a large spoon. Season to taste with salt. Serve immediately with corn chips and shots of the reserved juniper-flavored tequila.

# Texas Caviar

*Everything is bolder in Texas, just like this zesty guac: a trailer-park recipe for a rodeo-exciting flavor.*

2 large avocados, diced (about 2 cups)

Juice of 2 limes (about ¼ cup)

1 small green bell pepper, diced

¼ cup diced red onion

1 Roma tomato, diced

One 10-ounce can diced green chiles, drained

One 15-ounce can black-eyed peas with jalapeño peppers, drained and rinsed

½ cup zesty Italian salad dressing

Salt

Pepper

Hot sauce

**Flavored corn chips**

*Makes about 5 cups*

**In a medium bowl,** combine the avocados, lime juice, bell pepper, onion, tomato, chiles, and black-eyed peas with a large spoon. Drizzle the salad dressing over the top and mix well. Season to taste with salt, pepper, and hot sauce. Serve immediately with flavored corn chips.

# Fruity Salsa Guac

*A sweet and savory summertime surprise for even the most seasoned guac connoisseur. Avocados are special fruits, and this is a fruit salad worthy of them.*

2 large avocados, diced (about 2 cups)

Juice of 1 lime (about 2 tablespoons)

1 cup diced strawberries

½ cup diced cucumber

½ cup diced mango

¼ cup diced banana

1 teaspoon seeded and finely chopped jalapeño pepper

1 teaspoon honey

Salt

Pepper

**Unsalted (or low salt) blue corn tortilla chips or baked veggie chips**

*Makes about 3 ½ cups*

**In a medium bowl,** combine the avocados, lime juice, strawberries, cucumber, mango, banana, jalapeño, and honey with a large spoon. Season to taste with salt and pepper. Refrigerate in an airtight container for 2 to 12 hours. Serve with blue corn tortilla chips.

**Note:** This fruity guac is also delicious over ice cream, or as a topping for roasted pork, ham, or turkey.

# Guacamole de Poblanos

*This wonderfully warm, garlicky roasted poblano guac devastates all who dare to dip. It is a full-flavored ode to South American cooking. For a slightly spicier version, substitute the poblanos with* pasilla *chiles.*

2 medium, fresh poblano chiles (about 1 cup, chopped)

2 ripe Roma tomatoes

4 cloves garlic, unpeeled

2 large avocados, diced (about 2 cups)

Juice of 2 limes (about ¼ cup)

3 tablespoons chopped flat-leaf parsley

2 tablespoons finely crumbled *queso añejo* or other dry grating cheese, like Romano or Parmesan

4 slices radish, for garnish

**Tortilla chips**

*Makes about 3 ½ cups*

**Preheat the broiler.** Place the chiles, tomatoes, and garlic on a baking sheet. Slide the sheet 3 to 4 inches below the broiler. Roast, turning every few minutes, until soft and blistered (surfaces should have blackened spots), about 10 to 12 minutes. Place the chiles in a bowl, cover with a paper towel, and let cool for 5 minutes. Wipe away any blackened skin with a towel. Remove and discard the stems, seeds, and seed pods from the chiles and rinse. Peel and discard the tomato skins. Slip the papery skins from the garlic. In a food processor or blender, process the garlic and chile into a course purée. Spoon the puréed mixture into a large bowl. Chop the tomatoes and add to the purée. In a separate medium bowl, combine the avocados, lime juice, and parsley with a large spoon. Gently fold the avocado mixture into the chile-tomato mixture. Sprinkle with *queso añejo* and garnish with the radish slices. Serve immediately with tortilla chips.

# French Guac

*If the French ate guac (and surely they must, they just won't admit it), this would be how they made it.*

2 large avocados, diced (about 2 cups)

Juice from 2 limes (about ¼ cup)

¼ cup finely chopped cilantro

1 clove garlic, minced

¼ cup finely chopped red onion

¼ cup crumbled blue cheese, plus more for garnish

Salt

Pepper

**1 baguette, thinly sliced**

*Makes about 3¼ cups*

**In a medium bowl,** combine the avocados, lime juice, cilantro, garlic, red onion, and ¼ cup blue cheese with a large spoon. Season to taste with salt and pepper. Toast the baguette slices. Sprinkle a little blue cheese over the top for garnish. Serve the guacamole immediately with warm baguette toasts.

# Artichoke Guac

*Between the creamy feta and flavor-popping pine nuts, avocado and artichoke seem almost understated in this upscale taste-storm. Make this when you want to impress someone.*

2 large avocados, diced (about 2 cups)

Juice from 2 limes (about ¼ cup)

1 cup chopped marinated artichoke hearts

¼ cup toasted pine nuts

¼ cup chopped cilantro

Salt

Pepper

¼ cup crumbled feta cheese

**Tortilla chips**

*Make about 3 ¾ cups*

**In a medium bowl,** combine the avocados, lime juice, artichoke hearts, pine nuts, and cilantro with a large spoon. Season to taste with salt and pepper. Sprinkle the feta over the avocado mixture and serve immediately with tortilla chips.

# Cranberry Guac

*Cranberries boast a bursting, shameless taste, causing a vibrant collision with the creamy richness of avocado.*

⅔ cup fresh cranberries

2 large avocados, diced
(about 2 cups)

Juice from 2 limes (about ¼ cup)

½ cup salsa verde (store bought)

3 tablespoons finely chopped
cilantro

1 jalapeño pepper, seeded and
finely chopped

Garlic salt

**Tortilla chips**

*Makes about 3½ cups*

**Soak the cranberries** in hot water for 10 minutes. Meanwhile, in a medium bowl, combine the avocados, lime juice, salsa, cilantro, and jalapeño with a large spoon. Drain the cranberries and wipe off excess moisture with paper towels. Gently fold them into the avocado mixture. Season to taste with the garlic salt. Serve immediately with tortilla chips.

# Mediterranean Guac

*Strangers from foreign lands, hummus and avocado get along just fine. Toss in some smooth feta and sharp Kalamata olives, and your taste buds will be sailing on the cool, blue Mediterranean.*

2 large avocados, diced
(about 2 cups)

Juice from 1 lime (about
2 tablespoons)

½ cup plain hummus

¼ cup chopped cherry tomatoes

⅓ cup finely chopped cucumber

¼ cup pitted and chopped
Kalamata olives

¼ cup finely chopped red onion

¼ cup crumbled feta cheese

2 teaspoons balsamic vinegar

1 teaspoon chopped fresh oregano

Salt

Pepper

**Pita chips or toasted pita wedges**

*Makes about 3½ cups*

**In a medium bowl,** combine the avocados, lime juice, hummus, tomatoes, cucumber, olives, red onion, feta, vinegar, and oregano with a large spoon. Season to taste with salt and pepper. Serve immediately with pita chips.

*extreme guacs*

Avocados have long served as a sumptuous condiment to the finest foods. But here the roles are reversed. The entrée becomes the seasoning as guacamole rises to the occasion.

# Marinated Chicken Guac

## (People's Choice: 2007)

*Marinating the chicken overnight is essential here, as the bold flavoring of the warm, grilled chicken gets soothed by the avocado. Chop chicken straight off the grill and serve hot-n-cold style.*

Juice of 4 limes (about ½ cup)

3 cloves garlic, minced

4 teaspoons steak sauce

4 teaspoons Worcestershire sauce

Hot sauce

2 boneless chicken breast filets (about ½ pound)

2 large avocados, diced (about 2 cups)

1 lime, halved

Salt

Tortilla chips

*Makes about 3 cups*

**In a plastic resealable bag** (or a large mixing bowl), combine the lime juice, garlic, steak and Worcestershire sauces, and a dash of hot sauce for the marinade. Place the chicken breasts in the bag, turning them over to coat both sides. Seal the bag and refrigerate overnight. When ready to grill, remove the chicken breasts from the bag and discard the marinade. Grill for 20 to 30 minutes, turning over halfway through cooking time, until cooked through and golden brown. Remove the chicken from the grill, chop roughly into ½-inch cubes, and combine in a medium bowl with the avocados. Squeeze juice from the lime halves into the bowl and season to taste with salt. Mix well. Serve immediately with tortilla chips.

# Crab Guac

*Crabmeat and avocado were meant for each other, and this recipe proves it beyond a doubt. So simple and sublime, it's almost too good for a chip. Almost.*

2 large avocados, diced (about 2 cups)

Juice of 2 limes (about ¼ cup)

⅓ cup minced cilantro

1 tablespoon minced jalapeño pepper

½ cup minced red onion

½ cup finely chopped Roma tomato

2 cloves garlic, minced

1 teaspoon ground cumin

½ pound lump crabmeat, shells and cartilage sorted out

2 teaspoons extra-virgin olive oil

¼ teaspoon cayenne pepper

Salt

Pepper

**Tortilla chips**

*Makes about 4 cups*

**In a large bowl,** combine the avocados, lime juice, cilantro, jalapeño, onion, tomato, garlic, and cumin with a large spoon. In a separate bowl, combine the lump crabmeat with the olive oil, cayenne, and salt and pepper to taste. Lightly fold the crab mixture into the avocado mixture, taking care not to break apart the crabmeat. Adjust seasoning if necessary. Serve immediately in chilled martini glasses with tortilla chips.

# Turkey and Black Bean Chili with Guacamole

*Cool guacamole at the heart of a steaming bowl of chili is the greatest dipping pleasure known to man.*

TURKEY AND BLACK BEAN CHILI

1 teaspoon vegetable oil

½ pound lean ground turkey

¼ cup chopped white onion

2 cloves garlic, minced

1 carrot, chopped

1 jalapeño pepper, seeded and minced

1 tablespoon chili powder

1 teaspoon ground cumin

1 teaspoon dried oregano

⅛ teaspoon salt

One 28-ounce can stewed tomatoes

One 19-ounce can black beans, drained and rinsed

1 red bell pepper; chopped

2 cups guacamole (recipe follows)

**Tortilla chips**
***Makes about 4½ cups***

**In a large saucepan,** heat the oil over medium heat. Sauté the turkey, onion, garlic, carrot, jalapeño, chili powder, cumin, oregano, and salt, stirring occasionally, until the onion is soft, about 5 minutes. Stir in the tomatoes, black beans, and bell pepper. Cover and simmer for 40 minutes. Place the chili in a bowl and top with a scoop of guacamole. Serve with tortilla chips.

GUACAMOLE

2 large avocados, diced (about 2 cups)

Juice of 1 lime (about 2 tablespoons)

2 tablespoons chopped fresh cilantro

2 tablespoons minced red onion

Salt

Pepper

***Makes about 2 cups***

**In a medium bowl,** combine the avocados, lime juice, cilantro, onion, and salt and pepper to taste.

# Feta and Shrimp Cocktail Guac

*Classy and aesthetically gorgeous, this fresh take on the shrimp cocktail will turn heads and delight guests.*

2 large avocados, diced (about 2 cups)

Juice of 2 limes (about ¼ cup)

¼ cup crumbled feta cheese

¼ cup finely chopped cilantro

7 medium shrimp (3 chopped, and 4 whole for garnish), cooked

Salt

Pepper

Hot sauce

About ¼ cup shrimp cocktail sauce (store bought)

Tortilla chips

*Makes about 3 ½ cups*

**In a medium bowl,** gently fold the avocados, lime juice, feta, cilantro, and the chopped shrimp together with a large spoon. Season to taste with salt, pepper, and hot sauce. Lightly press the 4 whole shrimp neatly on top of the mixture. Carefully spoon the shrimp cocktail sauce over the top. Chill for 1 to 4 hours and serve with tortilla chips.

# Bacon Guac

*This guacamole is like a BLT that has escaped the shackles of bread and embraced the gorgeous green of avo-land. Just the smell of bacon cooking will have guests hovering in anticipation. Don't forget to hide some for yourself.*

2 large avocados, mashed (about 2 cups)

Juice of 2 limes (about ¼ cup)

¼ cup finely chopped cilantro

¼ cup finely chopped red onion

¼ cup finely chopped Roma tomato

Salt

Pepper

2 teaspoons olive oil

5 strips bacon

1 teaspoon Parmesan cheese, shredded

**Tortilla chips**

*Makes about 3 cups*

**In a medium bowl,** combine the avocados, lime juice, cilantro, red onion, and tomato with a large spoon. Season to taste with salt and pepper. Set aside. In a medium frying pan, heat the olive oil and fry the bacon until very crispy. Transfer to a paper towel–lined plate to drain. Crumble the bacon into small pieces, then stir into the avocado mixture. Season to taste with salt and pepper, then sprinkle with the shredded Parmesan. Serve with tortilla chips.

# Scarface Guac

*Cuban-style red beans and rice form a spicy, hot base for a chilly bowl of creamy guac. Say hello to my little friend.*

1 tablespoon extra-virgin olive oil

½ cup coarsely chopped red onion

2 cups water

½ cup brown rice

½ cup red beans

2 cloves garlic, minced

2 tablespoons cayenne pepper

2 large avocados, diced
    (about 2 cups)

Juice from 2 limes (about ¼ cup)

½ cup coarsely chopped cilantro

¼ cup seeded and finely chopped
    Fresno chile

¼ cup seeded and finely chopped
    Anaheim chile

Salt

Pepper

Hot sauce

**Tortilla chips**

*Makes about 4 cups*

**In a small pot,** heat the oil over medium heat. Add the red onion and sauté until softened, about 5 minutes. Add the water and bring to a boil. Add the brown rice, red beans, garlic, and cayenne and boil until the water boils off completely, about 15 to 20 minutes. Fluff the beans and rice and allow to set for 2 minutes. In a medium bowl, combine the avocados, lime juice, cilantro, and the Fresno and Anaheim chiles with a large spoon. Season to taste with salt, pepper, and hot sauce. Transfer the bean and rice mixture to a large bowl, then gently fold in the avocado mixture. Serve immediately with tortilla chips.

# Carne Asada Guac

*If you're making tacos, you might as well toss some carne asada into the guac. Cue the mariachis! The tequila marinade gives the meat a special bite.*

2 large avocados, mashed (about 2 cups)

Juice from 2 limes (about ¼ cup)

½ cup coarsely chopped cilantro

½ cup coarsely chopped red onion

10 ounces grilled chopped carne asada (recipe follows)

Salt

Pepper

Hot sauce

**Tortilla chips**

*Makes about 4 cups*

**In a medium bowl,** combine the avocados, lime juice, cilantro, red onion, and carne asada with a large spoon. Season to taste with salt, pepper, and hot sauce. Serve with tortilla chips.

MARINATED CARNE ASADA

1 tablespoon olive oil

½ cup tequila

½ cup lemon juice

½ cup lime juice

4 cloves garlic, crushed

1 medium onion, finely diced

½ teaspoon paprika

1 teaspoon pepper

Pinch of salt

2 to 4 pounds beef flap meat

*Makes about 2 cups*

**Combine all the ingredients** in a 1-pound resealable bag. Marinate in the refrigerator for 3 to 6 hours. Remove the beef from the marinade, discard the marinade, and grill for 10 to 15 minutes.

**Tip:** For quick carne asada, buy a taco from your local Mexican taqueria, then scoop out the meat into your guac.

# Lobster Guac

*From the depths of the sea to the shallows of your heart, lobster guac is the top shelf of guacamole extravagance. Treat yourself or someone you love.*

2 large avocados, diced
(about 2 cups)

Juice from 2 limes (about ¼ cup)

1 teaspoon finely chopped cilantro

1 teaspoon finely chopped
red onion

1 teaspoon seeded and minced
Anaheim chile

Salt

Pepper

4 ounces steamed lobster meat

Japanese pickled ginger, for garnish

**Sesame seed water crackers**

*Makes about 3 cups*

**In a medium bowl,** combine the avocados, lime juice, cilantro, red onion, and chile with a large spoon. Season to taste with salt and pepper. Gently fold in the lobster meat. Spoon into chilled martini glasses and garnish each glass with some of the pickled ginger. Serve with water crackers.

# Wonton Guac Bombs

*Make guac, not bombs. The chip and the guac merge entirely in this crispy yet luscious dipping bomb of the gods.*

2 large avocados, mashed
(about 2 cups)

Juice from 2 limes (about ¼ cup)

½ cup finely chopped cilantro

2 tablespoons curry powder

Salt

Pepper

20 wonton skins

Two 8-ounce packages cream
cheese cut into ¼-inch slices

Vegetable oil

Hot-and-sour dipping sauce
(store bought)

*Makes 20 wontons*

**In a medium bowl,** combine the avocados, lime juice, cilantro, and curry powder with a large spoon. Season to taste with salt and pepper. Set aside. On a moist cutting board or baking sheet, lay out the wonton skins. Put one generous teaspoon of guacamole in one corner of the skin. Place a thin slice of cream cheese onto the heaped guacamole. Brush the edges of the skin with water. Fold over into a triangle and press the edges gently to seal. Repeat with the remaining skins. Pour the vegetable oil into a medium frying pan, about ½ inch deep, and heat. Place the triangles, four to six at a time (depending on room), into the oil and fry until golden brown, about 1 to 2 minutes on each side. Place on a paper towel–lined plate to drain. Serve immediately with hot-and-sour dipping sauce on the side.

# Breakfast Guac

*Egg salad–style, bacon-infused guacamole makes an exciting wake-up call for the post-party sleepover crew. Serves up great with Bloody Marys (and hangovers).*

2 eggs, hardboiled and shelled

¼ cup mayonnaise

¼ cup finely chopped green onion

Paprika

Cayenne pepper

Black pepper

1 teaspoon olive oil

2 slices bacon

2 large avocados, diced
   (about 2 cups)

Salt

**Tortilla chips**

*Makes about 3 cups*

**Chop the eggs** and place in a medium bowl. Stir in the mayonnaise and green onion, and lightly season to taste with the paprika and the cayenne and black pepper. In a medium frying pan, heat the olive oil and fry the bacon until very crispy. Transfer to a paper towel–lined plate to drain. Crumble the bacon and then stir into the egg mixture. Gently fold in the avocados. Season to taste with salt. Serve immediately with tortilla chips.

# The DIY Guacamole Bar

*You can circumnavigate the organization of a proper Guac Off with this one final super-guac recipe and still inspire guacamole creativity in others. Guacamole bars are great for big parties like a housewarming, Oscar Night, or the Super Bowl.*

8 to 10 large avocados, diced

Juice from 4 to 5 limes (about 1 cup)

Salt

½ cup each chopped cilantro, red onion, and green onion

½ cup canned black beans, drained and rinsed

1 cup chopped tomato

¼ cup minced garlic

1 cup chopped Anaheim chile

½ cup each seeded and chopped jalapeño pepper, habanero chile, and poblano chile

½ cup chopped red bell pepper

½ cup chopped black olives

½ cup sour cream

1 cup each cooked and chopped carne asada and marinated chicken

½ cup cooked and chopped small shrimp

½ cup cooked crab meat

5 limes, halved

Hot sauce

Steak sauce

Cumin

Cayenne pepper

Crushed red pepper

Oregano

Pepper

**Tortilla and corn chips**

**In a large bowl,** combine the avocados and lime juice with a large spoon. Season to taste with salt. Place each of the other ingredients (as many as you want) in smaller bowls around the avocado mixture. Encourage your guests to create their own guacamole by scooping the basic avocado mixture into their bowls and adding fixings. Include an assortment of chips to sample your own guacamole, and whoever else's looks irresistible.

# guacamole road:
## the journey continues

Chocolate guacamole! Sitting bolt upright in the middle of the night, I'm squirting chocolate syrup over a bowl of chunky cubes of avocado in an over-guaced, half-asleep delusion. Still dazed, I think, "What else does it need?" A splash of milk? Or a squeeze of lime? Crisp sugar cookies for dipping? Is that guacamole? If it is—and I firmly believe so—then there is no end to this delightful green madness. Limitless guacamolebilities.

Here are some more guacamole ideas for all you culinary adventurers:

- **Banana and Blackberry Guac**
- **Basil Guac**
- **Berry Guac**
- **Black Bean Guac**
- **Cajun Guac**
- **Ceviche Guac**
- **Cherry Guac**
- **Chipotle–Goat Cheese Guac**
- **Curry Guac**
- **Goat Cheese Guac**
- **Kiwi Guac**
- **Papaya Guac**
- **Peach Guac**
- **Berry Guac**
- **Pesto Guac**
- **Pineapple Guac**
- **Salmon Guac**
- **Sausage Guac**
- **Sour Cream Guac**
- **Spicy-Hot Pepper Jack Cheese Guac**
- **Steak Sauce Gauc**
- **Sun-Dried Tomato Guac**

*. . . the possibilities are endless.*

# Concerning Mariachis

## GUAC OFF BONUS FEATURES

The ingredients of a great Guac Off are like the ingredients in guacamole—a mishmash mix of what's around, what's desirable, and what works. Whether you go all out on your Mexican theme with mariachis and sombreros, or simply run a half-time sideshow during your big game blowout, here are a few ideas you might consider to spice your bowl.

### VICTORY TEQUILA

The prize of a true Guac Off should always be a fine bottle of tequila—paying respect to the Aztec origins of competitions. One hundred percent pure blue agave tequila is produced only in the Mexican state of Jalisco, so your bottle should say, "100% de agave" and "Hecho en Mexico" somewhere on the label (never "Mixto," which means your tequila only contains 51 percent blue agave). Fine tequila is like fine wine, and may be chilled and sipped, instead of downed as shots, though a lick of salt and suck of lime is also a nice touch, even when sipping.

## THE REAL MARGARITA

Store-bought margarita mix is fine, but you haven't tasted a real margarita until you've squeezed fresh lime juice into a fine agave tequila with just a proper dash of triple sec for sweetness.

However much you're making, the ratio should be 2:1:1, tequila to lime juice to triple sec. So half the mixture will be made up of tequila, one quarter the fresh lime juice, and the final quarter triple sec. Mix it well with ice in a cocktail shaker. To get that delicious salt rim, wet the rim of a margarita glass with a lime wedge and turn the glass upside down into a shallow bowl (or a saucer) of coarse salt. Add ice to the glass, then carefully strain in the margarita.

## MARGARITA ALTERNATES

It makes sense that in an environment of creative guacamoles, a few inspired cocktails would fit right in. Margaritaville is a vast country just south of Guacamole-land, but here are a few ideas to get your creative juices flowing:

### The Ultimate Margarita

6 large limes, 2 cut into wedges

2 cups water

½ cup sugar

1 cup chilled 100 percent pure blue agave tequila

¼ cup orange liqueur

Coarse salt

*Makes 4 to 6 drinks*

*continued*

Peel the 4 whole limes and shred the peels into the water. Let stand for 30 minutes. Strain the lime-peel mixture through a sieve and discard the peels. Stir the sugar into the collected liquid until it dissolves. Squeeze the peeled limes into a small pitcher (should make about ½ cup juice), add the tequila, orange liqueur, and the sugar mixture. Wet the rims of the margarita glasses with a lime wedge, turn them upside down, then dip into a shallow bowl of coarse salt. Add ice to the glasses, and pour in the cocktail. Garnish with the lime wedges and reserve any leftover wedges for other use.

## Tequila Sunrise

1⅓ cups chilled orange juice

½ cup chilled 100 percent pure blue agave tequila

¼ cup chilled lime juice (about 2 limes)

2 tablespoons grenadine syrup

Kumquat slices (optional)

### Makes 4 drinks

In a pitcher, combine the orange juice, tequila, and lime juice. Pour over ice into four wine glasses. Slowly sink 1½ teaspoons grenadine syrup in each glass. Garnish with kumquat slices on wooden skewers, if desired.

## Sangria

1 cup orange juice

¼ cup lime juice (about 2 limes)

One 750 ml bottle dry red wine

¼ cup sugar

Orange slices

Lime slices

*Makes about 5 cups*

In a large pitcher, stir together the orange and lime juices. Add the wine and sugar. Stir until the sugar dissolves. Chill in the refrigerator for at least 5 hours. Serve garnished with orange and lime slices.

## MAKE YOUR OWN TORTILLA CHIPS

Making your own tortilla chips is supremely easy. Maybe not as easy as buying them, but the crafty purity of a homemade chip is something every guacamole lover should experience at least once in their career. And what better opportunity than your very own Guac Off to casually mention, "You like them? I made them myself."

Cut ten 8-inch flour or corn tortillas (corn tortillas are lower in fat) into wedges (the size is up to you, but keep them consistent). Brush the wedges with a thin coat of olive oil (about ¼ cup should do it). Sprinkle lightly with salt and cumin. Bake the wedges on a baking sheet at 350°F until golden brown, about 10 minutes. Store in an airtight container (no more than 2 to 3 days). Reheat in the microwave for 1 minute to serve hot.

## Other Chip Tips

- For garlic chips, stir 2 teaspoons fresh garlic into the oil before brushing the tortilla wedges and sprinkle crushed fresh garlic over them before baking.

*continued*

- For Parmesan chips, sprinkle Parmesan over the tortilla wedges before baking.

- For herb chips, stir 1 tablespoon dried crushed herbs into the oil before brushing the tortilla wedges.

No self-respecting Mexican would ever let another man make his taco. The best way to approach tacos is to set out all the ingredients—chopped, diced, shredded, and cooked—and let everyone build their own, just the way they like it. Cook and chop some marinated carne asada (page 86), shredded beef, and/or chicken. Warm some corn and flour tortillas. Lay out chopped tomatoes, olives, cilantro, onions, and shredded lettuce. Set aside small bowls of sour cream, salsa fresca (below), and, of course, plenty of guacamole.

### FRESH SALSA

Every superhero needs a sidekick, and fresh salsa is the perfect side dish to a tableful of guacs and tacos. Making fresh salsa can be almost as exciting and creative as guac-ing; here are a few standard recipes to get you started.

## Salsa Fresca

1½ cups finely chopped tomatoes

1 Anaheim pepper, seeded and finely chopped

¼ cup finely chopped green bell pepper

¼ cup chopped green onion

3 tablespoons chopped cilantro

Juice of 2 limes (about ¼ cup)

2 jalapeño peppers (or similar type), seeded and finely chopped

1 clove garlic, minced

Salt

Pepper

*Makes 3 cups*

In a medium bowl, mix together the tomatoes, Anaheim and bell peppers, green onion, cilantro, lime juice, jalapeños, and garlic with a wooden spoon. Season to taste with salt and pepper. Cover and chill for at least 1 hour before serving.

## Salsa Verde

6 to 8 fresh tomatillos, finely chopped (about 2 cups)

¼ cup chopped cilantro

2 tablespoons finely chopped red onion

1 fresh serrano pepper, seeded and finely chopped

¼ teaspoon sugar

2 tablespoons lemon juice

Salt

Pepper

*Make about 2 cups*

In a small bowl, stir together the tomatillos, cilantro, onion, serrano, sugar, and lemon juice with a wooden spoon. Season to taste with salt and pepper.

# Roasted Salsa

3 medium tomatoes, quartered

2 Fresno chiles, halved and seeded

1 tablespoon olive oil

½ onion, chopped

2 cloves garlic, minced

¼ teaspoon ground cumin

Salt

*Makes about 2 cups*

Remove the broiler pan, then preheat the broiler. Place the quartered tomatoes and Fresno chile halves, facedown, on the broiler pan, and slide it 4 inches below the heat. Broil for 10 minutes, or until the skins blacken and start to peel off. Remove from the broiler and let cool. Remove skins from the tomatoes and chiles and chop fine. In a small saucepan, heat the olive oil over medium-high heat and sauté the onion and garlic for about 3 minutes, or until softened. Stir in the tomatoes, chiles, and cumin. Simmer uncovered until the liquid has evaporated, about 10 minutes. Serve warm or chilled.

A group of jolly musicians hammering loud and lively Mexican music is as sweet and wonderful as Gummy Bears and Pop Rocks—and just like those candies, it's not something you want to overindulge in. This isn't a personal attack on mariachis—it's a metaphor for parties. After the food and guac are gone, after everyone has had some drinks and the sun has set and the kids are off to bed and the over-loud laughter is getting that slightly dangerous edge to it, it's time to stop tipping the guys with the instruments and let the Guac Off wind down. The beauty of starting a party midafternoon is that you've had a lovely time and you feel the end has come at a fairly decent hour. However, the danger of starting a party midafternoon is that by the early late hours, a few of the over-do-it types might be getting a bit too wild for their own good. Turn down the music. Put away the food. And clap the drunken winner on the back and tell him, "Nice job on your guacamole, friend. I can't wait to Guac Off with you again next year."

Sweep the chips from the porch. Dim the lights. And forget any of this ever happened.

After all, it's only guacamole.

# The Pit Crew

### FAREWELL AND THANK YOU FOR GUAC-ING

First and foremost, Jeremy and I must thank our beautiful and ever-supportive wives, Elaina Myers and Megan Webster, who lovingly hosted every event, carefully tasted every guac, and joyfully contributed to every element of this book.

Guac Offs are a celebration of community. And without the loving support of our own community of friends and family, this book would never have been possible. From contributing recipes and competing fiercely in our annual competitions to helping with photo shoots and editorial, this book is especially indebted to the following avocado-like individuals:

Malcolm and Mary Mattheson; Luke, Monica, and Elijah Fisher; Aaron Grasskopf; Jerry and Sue Samaniego; Jerry Samaniego; Jandi Swanson; Susanna Samaniego; Marilyn Myers; Jim Myers; Chata Samaniego; Terry Cornelius; Jeff "El Primero" Marcus; Garrett Francis; Matt Eason; Jacques Domerq; Tom Gomes; Dru Danforth; Devin Wilson; Stephanie Higgins; Suha Araj; Brie Cadman; Tyler Cornelius; Peter and Zia Lee; Matt and Jodi Warshaw; David Hedrick; Scott and Norma Miller; Ramon, Cory, Sarah, and li'l Ramon Samaniego; Chris and Lupe Kraus; Louie and Meg Samaniego; Joe Goss; Matt and Jenny Dito; Elwood; Evan Slater; Scott Chenoweth; Andre Aganza; Sarah Malarkey; Amy Treadwell; Sarah Billingsley; Suzanne LaGasa; Jane Chinn; Peter Perez; David Hawk; Doug Ogan; Linden Street Brewery; and the E-Street Café.

# Table of Equivalents

*The exact equivalents in the following tables have been rounded for convenience.*

## LIQUID/DRY MEASUREMENTS

| U.S. | Metric |
| --- | --- |
| ¼ teaspoon | 1.25 milliliters |
| ½ teaspoon | 2.5 milliliters |
| 1 teaspoon | 5 milliliters |
| 1 tablespoon (3 teaspoons) | 15 milliliters |
| 1 fluid ounce (2 tablespoons) | 30 milliliters |
| ¼ cup | 60 milliliters |
| ⅓ cup | 80 milliliters |
| ½ cup | 120 milliliters |
| 1 cup | 240 milliliters |
| 1 pint (2 cups) | 480 milliliters |
| 1 quart (4 cups, 32 ounces) | 960 milliliters |
| 1 gallon (4 quarts) | 3.84 liters |
| 1 ounce (by weight) | 28 grams |
| 1 pound | 448 grams |
| 2.2 pounds | 1 kilogram |

## LENGTHS

**U.S. Metric**

⅛ inch – 3 millimeters
¼ inch – 6 millimeters
½ inch – 12 millimeters
1 inch – 2.5 centimeters

## OVEN TEMPERATURE

| Fahrenheit | Celsius | Gas |
| --- | --- | --- |
| 250 | 120 | ½ |
| 275 | 140 | 1 |
| 300 | 150 | 2 |
| 325 | 160 | 3 |
| 350 | 180 | 4 |
| 375 | 190 | 5 |
| 400 | 200 | 6 |
| 425 | 220 | 7 |
| 450 | 230 | 8 |
| 475 | 240 | 9 |
| 500 | 260 | 10 |